Looking at Stars

Sun

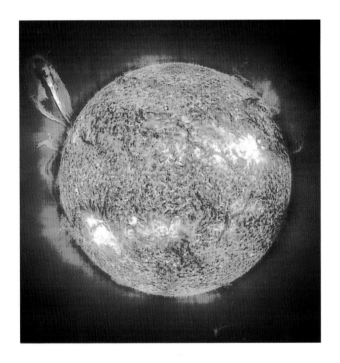

Robin Kerrod

Thameside Press

Distributed in the United States by
Smart Apple Media
1980 Lookout Drive
North Mankato, MN 56003

Text copyright © by Robin Kerrod 2001

Editor: Veronica Ross
Designer: Helen James
Illustrator: Chris Forsey
Consultant: Doug Millard
Picture researcher: Diana Morris

Printed in Hong Kong

Library of Congress Cataloging-in-Publication Data

Kerrod, Robin.
    Sun / written by Robin Kerrod.
        p. cm. -- (Looking at stars)
    Includes index.
    ISBN 1-930643-26-8
    1. Sun--Juvenile literature. [1. Sun.] I. Title.

QB521.5 .K47 2001
523.7--dc21   2001027272

9 8 7 6 5 4 3 2 1

Photo credits
Andrew Fruchter & the ERO team/NASA/Spacecharts: 29t.
M & C Denis-Huot/Still Pictures: 16bl.
Robin Kerrod: front cover, 1, 8bl, 8tr, 8-9bc, 9tr, 10bl, 11tl, 11cl, 11bl,
11br, 12tr, 14bl, 14cr, 15tl, 20bl, 31.
NASA/Spacecharts: 21br, 27cr, 30.
Private Collection/Bridgeman Art Library: 7b.
Royal Astronomical Society/Spacecharts: 19c.
Spacecharts: 4-5, 12b, 13t, 13bl,   20br, 21bl, 22, 29cr.
Karen Ward/Stockmarket/Corbis: 15tr.
Hui Yang, University of Illinois/NASA/Spacecharts: 24t

Contents

Introducing the Sun

From the Earth, we can see thousands of **stars** shining out of the darkness of the night sky. But there is one star that we can never see there. This star appears in the sky during the daytime. In fact, it brings us daytime—the time when it is light.

This daytime star is the star we call the Sun. It is our local star. It looks very much bigger and very much brighter than the other stars only because it is very much nearer to us

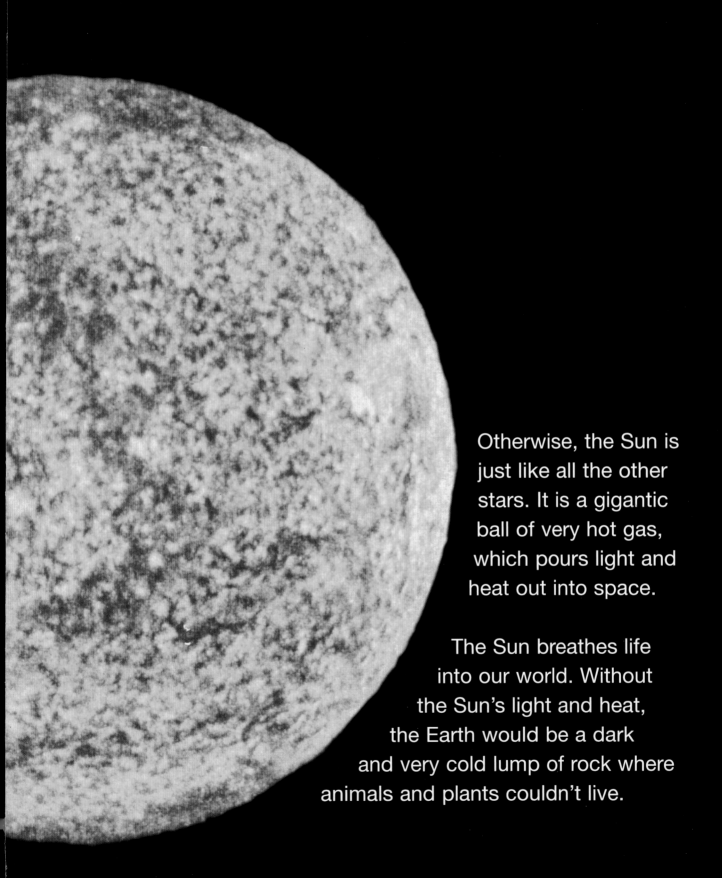

Otherwise, the Sun is
just like all the other
stars. It is a gigantic
ball of very hot gas,
which pours light and
heat out into space.

The Sun breathes life
into our world. Without
the Sun's light and heat,
the Earth would be a dark
and very cold lump of rock where
animals and plants couldn't live.

Sun in the sky

The Sun appears in the sky every morning. It rises, or climbs into the sky, in the east. This time is called sunrise or dawn. During the morning, the Sun climbs higher and higher into the sky, traveling towards the west. It reaches its highest point at midday, or noon.

The setting Sun

In the afternoon, the Sun sinks lower and lower in the sky. Finally, it sets, or drops below the horizon, in the west. After sunset, the sky becomes dark. Night falls. The sky stays dark until the Sun rises the next morning.

△ Ra's boat
The ancient Egyptians thought that their god Ra carried the Sun across the sky every day in a boat.

◁ The rising Sun
Every morning the Sun appears to rise in the east. It passes through the sky, setting in the west in the evening.

East   West

6

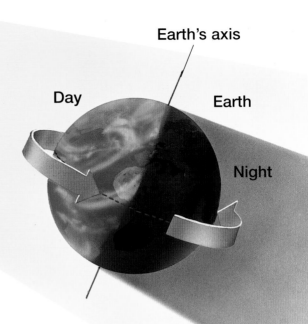

Sun

Earth's axis

Day

Earth

Night

Spinning round

Every day we see the Sun move through the sky. It seems to be circling the Earth. But the Sun is not moving, it is us. The Earth spins round in space, making it look as if the Sun moves in circles around the Earth.

△ **The spinning top**

The Earth spins round in space like a top. It spins around an imaginary line called the axis.

In the sunlight, people and trees throw dark shadows on the ground. Shadows move as the Sun moves across the sky.

◁ **Shadow time**

*People used to tell the time of day with a **sundial**. The position of the pointer's shadow on the dial showed the time.*

Lighting our world

The Sun produces huge amounts of energy. It gives off much of this energy as light, which we can detect with our eyes. Light beams travel very fast. They take about 8 ½ minutes to travel to us from the Sun, 93 million miles (150 million kilometers) away. The energy in sunlight gives life to the Earth. Plants use the energy to make their food.

△ **Seeing red**
Why does this beautiful hibiscus flower look red? The reason is that red is the only color in sunlight that the flower reflects, or sends back, into our eyes.

Light for life
Like all plants, these giant redwood trees use sunlight to make food in their green leaves. Redwoods are the biggest plants on Earth, growing to over 330 feet (100 metres) tall.

▽ Over the rainbow

We see all the colors that make up sunlight in a rainbow. The main ones are violet, indigo, blue, green, yellow, orange, and red.

▷ Blue skies

Clear, sunny skies are usually blue. The tiny air particles scatter more blue light into our eyes than any other color. This tower is a special telescope for studying the Sun.

▽ Setting Sun

At sunset, the sky often turns a beautiful orange. This happens when dust in the air stops other colors getting through.

Rainbow colors

Sunlight seems to be white or colorless. But in fact it is a mixture of many colors. We can see these colors in a rainbow. Rainbows form when raindrops split up white light into its colors, from violet to red.

We see objects in different colors because of what happens when sunlight falls on them. They absorb (take in) some colors and reflect (send back) others. We see objects in the colors they reflect.

Into the shadows

When you stand in sunlight, you cast a shadow on the ground. The Moon casts a shadow in space, too.

From time to time, the Moon's shadow falls on the Earth's surface. This happens when the Sun, the Moon, and the Earth line up exactly in space. From the Earth, we see the Moon pass in front of the Sun and cover it up. This is an **eclipse** (covering-up) of the Sun. Eclipses take place once every year or two.

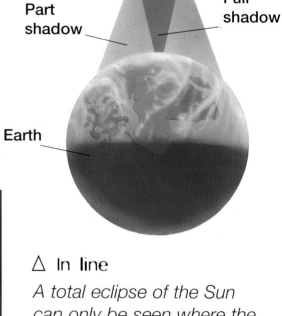

Sun

Moon

Full shadow

Part shadow

Earth

▽ Eclipse in Hawaii
The sky darkens in Hawaii during the total eclipse of July 11, 1991. An orange glow lights up the horizon.

△ In line
A total eclipse of the Sun can only be seen where the full shadow of the Moon touches the Earth.

△ **Fiery fountains**

The Moon has covered the face of the Sun. Little red fountains of gas, called prominences, appear around the edge of the Moon.

▽ **Europe's eclipse, 1999**

Clouds spoiled the total eclipse on August 11.

Moon shadow

The Moon's shadow only ever covers a tiny area of the Earth's surface. Only people inside this area experience darkness, or total eclipse. Outside this area, people see the Moon cover only part of the Sun. This is a partial eclipse.

A total eclipse is very exciting. One moment the Sun is shining. The next moment the Moon covers the Sun, and day turns into night. But darkness lasts for only a few minutes. Then the Moon moves on and uncovers the Sun. Day returns once more.

▽ **Night at noon**

It is nearly noon, but it is as dark as midnight.

▽ **Day returns**

The Moon moves on and uncovers the Sun.

Invisible sunlight

The Sun gives off energy as light rays we can see. And it also gives off energy as rays we can't see. We can feel some invisible rays when we stand in the sunlight. They are heat rays, which warm our bodies. Their proper name is infrared rays.

We can't see or feel the other rays the Sun gives off. But some do affect us. Ultraviolet rays make our skin turn brown. If we stay too long in the sunlight, they will burn us.

The Sun also gives off radio waves. Astronomers pick up the Sun's radio signals using special telescopes.

△ Suntan
The Sun's ultraviolet rays tan our bodies when we sunbathe.

▽ Telling tails
*The invisible **solar wind** makes comets grow tails.*

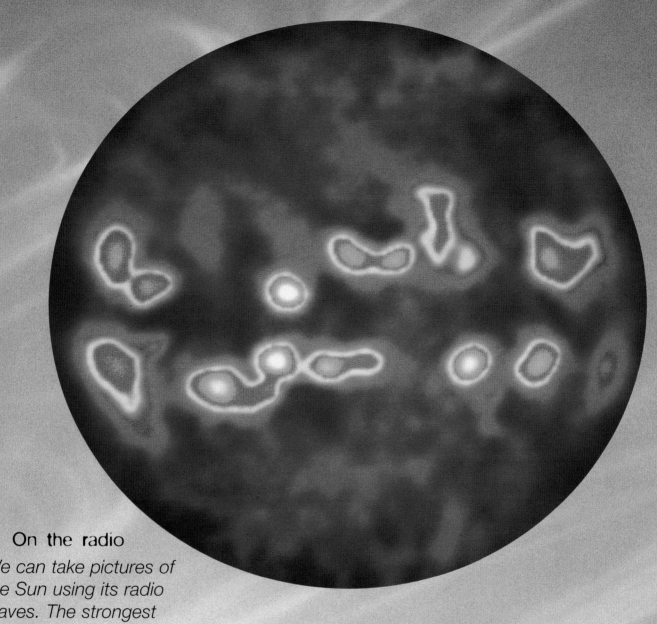

▷ On the radio

We can take pictures of the Sun using its radio waves. The strongest waves come from spots in the middle.

Solar wind

The Sun also gives off streams of electric particles. They form a "wind" that blows into space, causing electrical storms on Earth.

◁ Big dishes

Astronomers *pick up the Sun's radio waves using radio telescopes.*

Warming our world

The invisible heat rays that come from the Sun make our world a warm and comfortable place for millions of species (kinds) of animals and plants.

The Sun's heat brings about changes in the air, called the weather. It warms up the air and sets it moving, as the wind. It heats up the water in rivers and seas and turns it into vapor (gas). High in the air, the vapor cools and forms clouds of little water drops. These drops grow, then fall as rain or snow.

▽ **In the desert**
Only a few plants, like the Joshua tree, can grow in the hot, dry Mojave Desert in California.

◁ **In the tropics**
Clouds gather over the hills in tropical Hawaii. Plants grow well in the hot, moist climate.

▽ In temperate regions

Buffalo graze among the conifer trees in the cool Rocky Mountains of North America. Heavy snow falls in winter.

Equator

△ At the pole

Snow and ice are always found near the North Pole. It is too cold for plants to grow, but some animals live there.

Climates

Different parts of the world have varying temperatures and rainfall. We say they have different **climates**.

The hottest climates are found near the Equator, around the middle of the Earth. The climate cools down north or south of the Equator. The Sun is lower in the sky and sends down weaker rays. The coldest climates are at the North and South Poles.

The tilting Earth

In most parts of the world, the temperature and the weather change gradually as the months go by. The lengths of the days and nights change, too. The same changes take place every year, dividing the year into periods of time called seasons. In many parts of the world there are four seasons—summer, fall, winter, and spring. Summer is the hottest, winter the coldest, with fall and spring in between.

▷ **The four seasons**
The dates mark the beginning of summer, fall, winter, and spring in northern parts of the world.

June 21

△ **Summer**
Days are long and warm. Plants are flowering and making seeds.

◁ **Wet and dry**
The hot grasslands of East Africa have only two seasons—wet and dry.

◁ **Spring**
Days are lengthening and warming up. Buds and shoots are appearing.

March 21

December 21

Sun

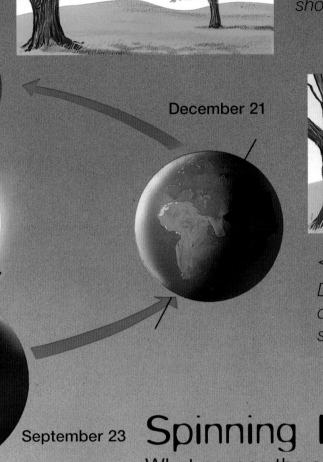

◁ **Winter**
Days are short and cold. Many trees have shed their leaves.

September 23

△ **Fall**
Days are shortening and cooling down. Fruits are ripe, and growth slows down.

Spinning like a top

What causes the **seasons**? It is the way the Earth travels around the Sun every year. As it travels, it spins round (see page 7). But it does not spin in an upright position. Its axis is tilted. This means that a place on Earth tilts more towards the Sun at some times of the year than at others. The more a place tilts towards the Sun, the warmer it is. The more it tilts away from the Sun, the cooler it is.

Star of the day

To us, the Sun is a special star. It brightens our days and keeps us and all living things alive. But as stars go, the Sun is very ordinary. There are millions of stars like it in the night sky.

The Sun is over 100 times bigger across than the Earth. If the Earth were the size of a pea, the Sun would be bigger than a beach ball.

The Sun is quite different from the Earth. The Earth is a ball of rock, while the Sun is a great ball of very hot gas.

It contains many different substances, or chemical elements. The main ones are hydrogen and helium. But it also contains heavier elements, such as carbon and iron.

▽ Island of stars
*The Sun and all the other stars in the night sky belong to a great star island in space called a **galaxy**. From a distance, it would look just like this one.*

SUN FACTS
Distance from Earth:
93,000,000 miles
(150,000,000 km)
Diameter: 875,000 miles
(1,400,000 km)
Mass: 333,000 times Earth's mass
Surface temperature: 10,000°F
(5,500°C)
Inside temperature:
27,000,000°F (15,000,000°C)
Spins round in: 25 days

▽ **Among the stars**
*A spacecraft named SOHO
took this picture of the Sun
against a background of stars.*

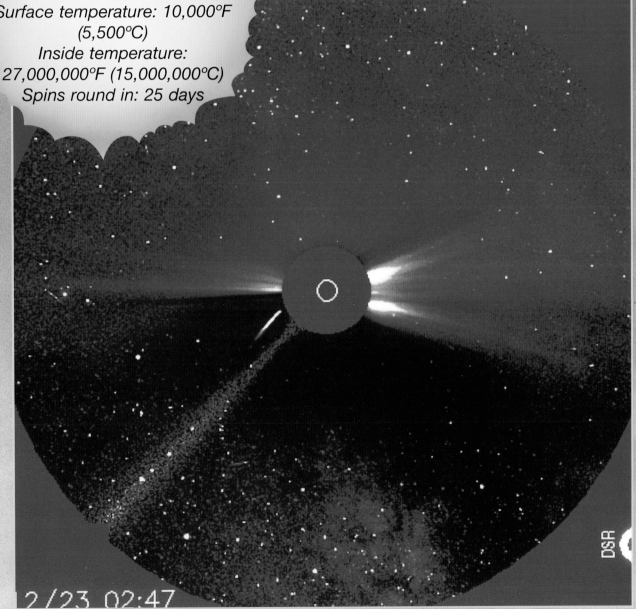

2/23 02:47

DSR

The Sun is incredibly hot. In the center, temperatures reach millions of degrees.

This is where the Sun produces the fantastic amounts of energy that keep it shining.

The dazzling Sun

The Sun is made up of a number of layers, but we can only ever see the top layer. This is the photosphere, which means "light ball." This layer produces the light and other rays that stream from the Sun. Beneath the photosphere there is a deeper layer in which currents of gas rise and fall. The rising currents carry hot gas from deep inside the Sun up to the surface where it gives off its heat. Then the gas cools down and sinks. This process makes the Sun's surface boil and bubble.

▽ **Bright face**

The face of the Sun is glaring white. This bright face is called the photosphere.

▽ **In close-up**

In special telescopes, the Sun's surface looks speckled. This happens because it is boiling.

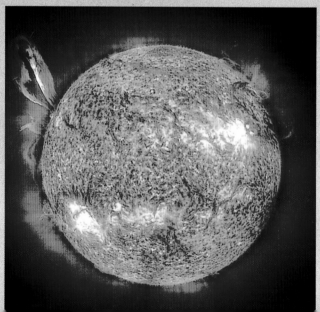

Outer layers

The Sun also has outer layers, which form its atmosphere. Usually, we can't see the atmosphere because of the glare of the Sun's face. We can see it only during a total eclipse, when the Sun's face is covered up.

The first layer of atmosphere is pink, and is called the chromosphere. The outer layer is called the corona.

Warning!

Never look at the Sun directly with your eyes. It is so bright that it will damage your eyes and may blind you.

▽ **The Sun's crown**
The Sun's outer atmosphere, called the corona, or "crown," billows out into space.

▽ **Solar ripples**
Ripples spread out over the Sun's surface after a kind of explosion called a sunquake.

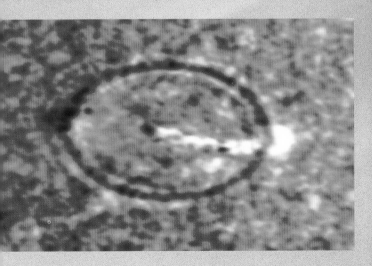

Stormy Sun

From Earth, the Sun looks much the same all the time, a yellowish-white glaring ball. But through their telescopes and other instruments, astronomers find that the Sun's surface is constantly changing.

Sometimes very bright areas appear on the surface, called **flares**. They are powerful explosions that blast particles into space and make the solar wind blow fiercely. Sometimes dark blotches appear, called sunspots. They appear dark because they are cooler than the rest of the surface.

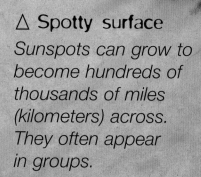

△ Spotty surface
Sunspots can grow to become hundreds of thousands of miles (kilometers) across. They often appear in groups.

◁ Flaming tongue
A huge tongue of fiery gas hundreds of times bigger than the Earth shoots out from the Sun's surface into space.

△ Looping the loop

Around the Sun's edge,
great streamers of flaming
gas hurtle high above
the surface. Called
prominences, they
often form loops like this.

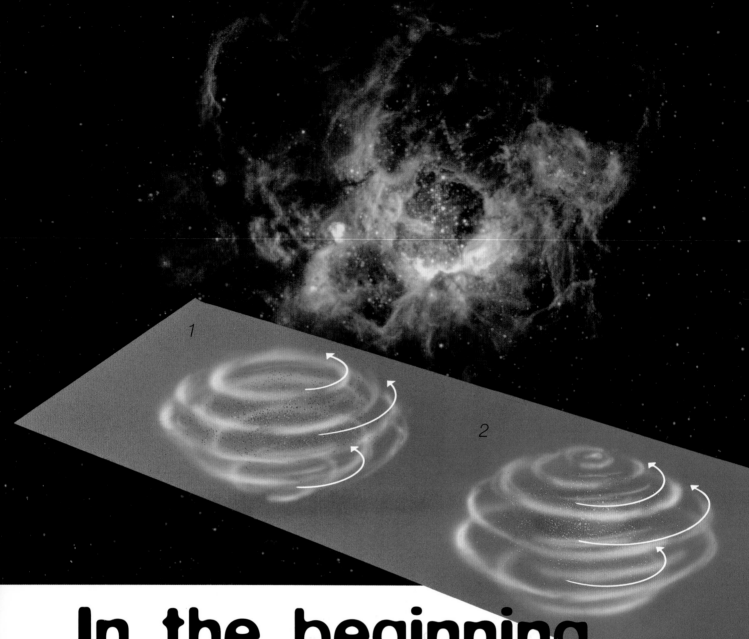

1

2

In the beginning

Every day the Sun rises and brings us light and warmth. The Sun has been shining as it does today for a long, long time—but has there always been a Sun? The answer is no.

About 5,000 million years ago, the Sun did not exist. In the part of space where we now live there was nothing but a great cloud of gas and dust. In this cloud the Sun was born.

◁ Billowing clouds

Great clouds of wispy gas, called nebulas, are found in spaces between the stars.

▽ The Sun is born

Four stages in the birth of the Sun:

1 A cloud of gas and dust starts to collapse. It begins to spin round.

2 The more it shrinks, the hotter it gets inside.

3 In time, the hot part inside becomes a ball. It is the infant Sun. Other material flattens out around it to form a disk.

3

4 The Sun begins shining, and material in the disk gathers together to form the planets.

Heating up

One day, the particles of gas and dust in the cloud started to attract one another. This happened because of **gravity**, the pull all things have on one another.

As the particles came together, the cloud began shrinking. At the same time it began heating up and spinning round. After millions of years, the center became a hot ball and began to shine brightly as the Sun. Meanwhile, bits of colder material had formed a disk around the Sun. These bits eventually grew into the **planets**.

4

The Sun's family

Years ago, people thought that the Earth was the center of the Universe. They thought that the Sun circled the Earth. But we now know that it is the other way round. The Earth circles the Sun.

The Earth is a body called a planet. Eight other planets circle the Sun. The planets are the most important members of the Sun's family in space, which we call the **Solar System**.

▷ Nine planets

These are the planets in the order in which they circle the Sun. The pictures show what they look like, but they are all different sizes.

Asteroids
Small chunks of rocks

Mars
A small planet with a noticeable red color

Venus
The planet that comes closest to Earth

Earth
Our home planet, and the only one that teems with life

Mercury
The fastest planet, closest to the Sun

Saturn
Another gas giant, circled by shining rings

Neptune
A twin of Uranus, with a beautiful blue color

Pluto
The farthest and tiniest planet, smaller than our Moon

Jupiter
The giant among planets, a great gas ball

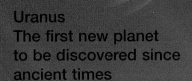

Uranus
The first new planet to be discovered since ancient times

Comets and asteroids

Many other smaller bodies belong to the Solar System. They include the moons that circle many of the planets, and the smaller asteroids found between Mars and Jupiter. Smaller still are icy lumps that we see in the night sky as **comets**.

The Sun is hundreds of times bigger than all of these bodies put together and holds onto them with its powerful pull, called gravity.

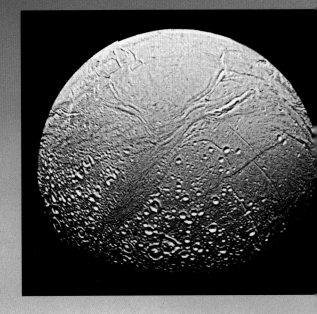

△ **One of many moons**
Most planets have moons circling around them. This is an icy moon of Saturn called Enceladus.

End of the story

The Sun was born nearly 5,000 million years ago, and it has been shining ever since. Astronomers think that it will carry on shining for about another 5,000 million years. Then it will start to die.

The Sun will not suddenly fizzle out and stop shining. It will die slowly over millions of years. Gradually the Sun will swell up and become redder in color. It will get bigger and bigger. In time, it will probably swallow up the planet Mercury, which will melt and turn to gas. By then, the Sun will be more than 50 times bigger than it is now. It will have become a kind of star called a red giant.

▽ Baking time
The heat from the swollen, dying Sun will one day bake the Earth and turn it into a lifeless ball of cracked rock.

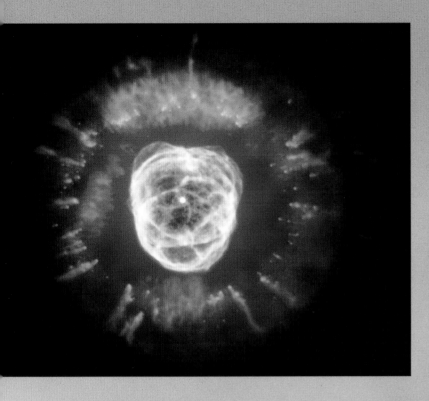

◁ **A dying sun**

A dying star puffs off rings of gas as it dies. We see them as a cloud, or nebula. It is easy to see why this one is called the Eskimo nebula.

▽ **White dwarfs**

A cluster of white dwarfs (circled) in space. They were once big and bright like the other stars in the picture.

Into the darkness

One day, the giant Sun will start to shrink again. Eventually it will become a tiny body not much bigger than the Earth, called a white dwarf. Millions of years later, its light will fade and it will become a black dwarf. It will disappear forever into the darkness of space.

Harnessing the Sun

Most of the energy we use comes from burning fuels, such as oil, gas, and coal. But one day these fuels will run out. Then we shall have to rely more on other sources of energy

One is solar power, or the energy the Earth receives from the Sun. Every day, the Sun beams down more energy than we will ever need.

We can harness the Sun's energy in two ways. One is to collect it using glass panels or mirrors. Some solar power stations use thousands of mirrors and turn solar energy into electricity.

Another way of harnessing the Sun's energy is with **solar cells**. These are little crystals that turn sunlight into electricity. But panels of thousands of cells are needed to produce enough power. They are used to power spacecraft.

◁ *The long "wings" that sprout from the Russian space station Mir are panels of solar cells.*

Useful words

astronomer A person who studies the stars and all the other heavenly bodies.

climate The usual weather a place has during the year.

comet An icy lump that starts to glow when it nears the Sun.

eclipse of the Sun The moment when the Moon passes in front of the Sun and casts a shadow on the Earth.

flare A violent explosion on the Sun's surface.

galaxy A great star "island" in space containing many billions of stars.

gravity The pull that every lump of matter has on every other lump.

planet A large body that circles the Sun.

season A period of the year when the weather is much the same as in previous years.

solar To do with the Sun.

solar cell A device that changes light into electricity.

Solar System The Sun's family, including the planets, their moons, and comets.

solar wind A stream of particles given out by the Sun.

star A huge ball of very hot gases in space.

sundial A kind of clock, which measures time by the position of shadows on a dial.

Index